Williamson W Publishing

KIDS' EASY BIKE CARE

Tune-Ups, Tools & Quick Fixes

STEVE COLE

ILLUSTRATIONS BY SARAH RAKITIN

Quick Starts for Kids!

WILLIAMSON PUBLISHING CHARLOTTE, VERMONT

Library of Congress Cataloging-in-Publication Data

Cole, Steve, 1975-
    Kids' easy bike care : tune-ups, tools & quick fixes / Steve Cole.
        p. cm. -- (Quick starts for kids!)
    Includes index.
    Summary: A guide to maintaining a bicycle in good operating condition including step-by-step tune-up instructions, a before-every-ride safety checklist, preparing an emergency kit, and making simple roadside repairs.
    ISBN 1-885593-86-4
    1. Bicycles--Maintenance and repair--Juvenile literature. [1. Bicycles--Maintenance and repair.] I. Title. II. Williamson quick starts for kids! book.

TL430.C64 2003
629.28'772--dc21

2003043090

Quick Starts for Kids!® series editor: **Susan Williamson**
Project editor: **Vicky Congdon**
Interior design and illustrations: **Sarah Rakitin**
Cover design: **Marie Ferrante-Doyle**
Cover illustrations: **Michael Kline**
Printing: **Quebecor World**

Photography: page 22: Lance Armstrong, © Cor Vos at www.corvos.nl; page 23: mountain biker at World Cup, © Mark Dawson/fattirefotos.com

Williamson Publishing Co.
P.O. Box 185
Charlotte, VT 05445
(800) 234-8791

Printed in Canada

10 9 8 7 6 5 4 3 2 1

Dedication

In memory of my father, Jack Cole. His strength and courage were inspirational to us all.

Acknowledgments

Many thanks to Sarah Rakitin, whose patience and support helped to make this book possible. I'd also like to thank Bret Hamilton for his time and expertise and Vicky Congdon for her hard work and attention to detail.

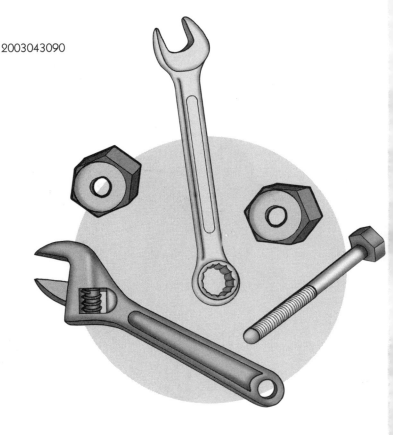

CONTENTS

LET'S HIT THE ROAD!

Riding a bike is a blast! The wind whistling past your helmet, the quiet whiz of the tires, and the feeling of freedom as you cruise along on your own wheels all make biking super cool! And now you can be in charge of taking care of those wheels, too. Tuning up your own bike — performing basic maintenance and simple repairs — is very satisfying. When your bike is in top shape, it performs at its best (it's safer, too), and it's just plain more fun to ride it!

My father and I began performing simple maintenance tasks on my bike when I was about eight years old. We'd head down to his basement workshop where he'd show me how to adjust my brakes and "lube" my chain when it was dirty or squeaky. I installed my own water-bottle holder and even learned how to fix a flat tire. I remember thinking how awesome it was that now I could keep my own bike in tip-top shape — and I didn't have to wait for my dad to help me out!

I'd like to share that feeling of accomplishment with you. I'll take you step-by-step through a basic tune-up and even show you some simple emergency repairs you can make along the road. It's important to learn what repairs and adjustments you can safely do at home and what work needs to be done at a bike repair shop. I'll also review the rules of the road and recommended riding techniques.

I hope you enjoy reading and using this book as much as I did writing it. Here's to many hours of cycling fun on a well-maintained bike!

Steve Cole

KIDS' TOP QUESTIONS ABOUT BIKING . . . WITH ANSWERS!

1) My brakes squeal when I put them on. Is this dangerous?

Squeaky or squealing brakes are not necessarily dangerous, but you should check them out to make sure that your brakes are set up properly (it will make your ride quieter, too!). See page 42 to find out more about how the brakes and rims (the metal wheels) should be set up. If you've adjusted them and they're still making noise, see page 46.

2) My parents made me put a bell on my bike, but it's embarrassing because none of my friends have one. Why do I need it? Would it be OK to remove it?

Bells and horns are important pieces of safety equipment, especially if you're riding on a sidewalk or bike path. They're an effective way for you to let a pedestrian, cyclist, or roller blader in front of you know that you are coming up from behind and would like to get by. The sound of a bell or a horn is more distinctive than your voice, plus it carries farther. So, I definitely wouldn't recommend removing it.

But why not make your bell more fun to have on your bike? If it's metal, use permanent magic markers to color it. You can also use glitter, puffy or acrylic paints, stickers, or decals to jazz it up.

3) I am saving up to buy my own bike. Should I consider a used bike or buy a new one at a bike shop?

The bottom line is how much do you want to spend (and for how long do you want to save)? You can find a great value in a used bike (and it often means you can afford a much nicer brand or model). If you're buying it from an individual (through a classified ad in the paper, for example), I recommend having a bike shop evaluate its condition.

Whether you're considering new or used, the best place to start your research is the bike shop. You can learn what's new in terms of bike *components* (special parts or features). (If you see something you like on a new bike, you can usually add it to a used bike too!) Have a salesperson fit you properly with a bike. That way, whether you buy a new or used bike, you'll know how the fit should feel. Take the bike for a short spin, paying attention to how easily it shifts and brakes and to the general feel of a well-maintained bike. These important points will help you evaluate the condition of a used bike, too.

4 I always get hand—me—down stuff from my older brother, including his old bike. It doesn't seem fair. How can I jazz up this bike and make it feel like mine?

If you've inherited an older bike (or just want to give yours a new look), you can customize it by adding flashy stickers or decals to the frame. Automotive pinstriping tape (from an auto supply store) makes great racing stripes. Decorative plastic pieces (specially made for bike wheels) attached to the spokes will give you some eye-catching wheels. Then, choose some fun, new accessories (page 60) to go on your "new" bike.

5 I'm 13 years old and I live in a city. My parents won't let me ride in the street without an adult, and it's illegal to ride on the sidewalk. All my friends are allowed to ride in traffic, so I can't go anywhere with them. Is there any way I can show my parents that I'm a responsible rider?

Your parents ultimately make these kinds of decisions with you because they know you, and they know the traffic conditions near where you live. If I were you, I would show my parents how much I know about riding in traffic, such as the rules of the road and hand signals. I would remind them that I wear my helmet whenever I go biking. And, I would tell them exactly where and when I plan to ride. Then, ask your parents again how they feel about this issue. If they still say no, then that's the decision until you get a little older. (Remember, they are not setting these rules to punish you, but rather to keep you safe. And there are definitely places where no one — at any age — should be biking.) Meanwhile, ask if they could drive you (with your bike) to a park or bike path where you can meet your friends.

Do I really need my bike helmet every time I ride? It's just a short ride to my friend's house a few streets away. And can I wear the football helmet that I already own? Or do I need to buy a real bike helmet?

OK, you'll hear me say this more than once in this book: A bike helmet is the most important piece of safety equipment you can use while riding a bike. Accidents don't just happen on roads — they happen on sidewalks, in driveways, and on bike paths. And most bike accidents happen close to home, on those "short rides." You don't have to be riding very fast to hurt your head, and a head injury can be very serious. A helmet provides critical protection for your skull in case of impact.

And no, please don't wear your football helmet (or any other non-biking helmet) when you're riding your bike! Bike helmets are designed specifically for the type of injury that could occur in a biking accident. They're not expensive — and they're worth every penny!

For information on choosing and using the proper helmet, including ensuring the right fit, see pages 8 to 10.

My chain falls off frequently when I switch gears. Is there anything I can do?

Make sure that your chain, chain ring, and sprocket (see pages 24 and 26 to learn where these parts are) are free of dirt and grease buildup. They should have a metallic shine. If they look dark and greasy, follow the steps for cleaning and lubing them (pages 40 to 41).

If this maintenance doesn't help, try adjusting the front and rear derailleurs (page 58). If it's still not better, have the bike checked out at a bike repair shop.

SAFETY FIRST!

A responsible bike rider always puts safety first. That means dressing appropriately, always giving your bike a quick safety check before heading off (my checklist on page 16 makes it quick and easy!), and knowing the rules of the road so you can share the space safely and courteously with pedestrians, other bikes, and vehicles.

THE ALL·IMPORTANT HELMET

The most important piece of biking equipment you can own is a helmet. You should wear a helmet *whenever you ride your bike.* You know how much it can hurt to bang your head on something. Well, imagine banging your head while riding your bike at full speed! Ouch! That's why helmets are so critical for *everyone* to wear. They come in some really wild and wacky designs, so it's fun to pick one out. A rounded, smooth design protects you more effectively than a style with lots of plastic ridges and projections or points that could snag on something.

FOR MORE INFO ON HELMETS ...

Is wearing a bike helmet required by law where you live? Many states have laws requiring bicycle helmet use. To find out about your state, contact the Bicycle Helmet Safety Institute at <**www.bhsi.org**>.

The National SAFE KIDS Campaign often sponsors community bike safety promotions that include selling helmets at very reasonable prices. You'll find contact information for your state's coalition and coordinators at <**www.safekids.org**>.

FITTING A HELMET

The most important thing you can do to ensure that your helmet works effectively is to make sure it fits properly. If you wear a helmet that is too large, it will simply slide backward if you bang your head and won't provide any protection. A helmet that is too small won't protect you in critical locations like your forehead.

Here's how to check for proper fit:

1. Put on your helmet and buckle the chin strap. It should feel snug but not too tight. Release the strap and have a friend or family member help you adjust it if necessary.

2. Make sure the helmet doesn't block your vision in any direction. Put your hands on top of the helmet and try to move it forward, backward, and sideways. If the helmet moves easily in *any* of these directions, it's too big.

If your helmet moves this far in any direction, it doesn't fit properly and won't protect you.

3. Readjust the straps. If you can still move the helmet back and forth, add padding to the inside. Padding usually comes with a new helmet or you can buy some at a bike shop. Bring your helmet along to the shop so that you can determine whether the fit can be corrected with padding alone. If the helmet fits loosely even with padding, it's probably too big for you. The salespeople can fit you with a new one.

As long as my helmet still fits, can I just keep using the same one?

I hope you never have to replace your helmet for this reason, but if you have a bike accident wearing your helmet, you'll need to get a new one. A helmet provides a foam barrier against your head. This foam is designed to compress so it, rather than your skull, absorbs the impact of a fall. Once a helmet absorbs an impact, the foam may already be compressed, which means the helmet no longer provides as much protection. You can't tell by looking at it whether or not it's damaged. So to be on the safe side, replace it.

THE WELL·DRESSED CYCLIST

🚲 Wear brightly colored clothes while biking so that motorists, pedestrians, and other bicyclists can see you.

🚲 If you're wearing baggy pants or bell-bottoms, be sure to roll up the cuff on the chain side or put a band around the pant leg so it doesn't get caught on the sprockets.

🚲 Watch for loose or untied shoelaces that might get caught in a part of the bike while you're pedaling. Don't tie your sweatshirt or sweater around your waist — the sleeves dangle down while you ride, and if they get caught in the spokes or chain, you'll go flying! Store extra clothing in a backpack or handlebar bag (page 61) instead.

QUICK STARTS TIPS!™

Protect your eyes

To ride more safely and comfortably, wear sunglasses to help with glare and keep the wind away from your eyes. They also protect your eyes from stray pebbles or bugs (yuck!).

SAFETY ACCESSORIES

LIGHTS AND REFLECTORS

Don't ride your bike at night — it's too dangerous. Also, avoid riding at dusk or very early in the morning, because it's difficult for motorists, as well as pedestrians and other cyclists, to see you. If you must travel at those times of day, please be sure you use or wear the following safety equipment. And if you're not properly equipped, call home for a ride!

Reflective vest. It has strips of material that reflect car headlights.

Backpack reflector. If you'll be wearing a backpack while you ride, attach a plastic reflector, a light (see below) or strips of reflective material to it.

Reflectors. Your bike should have one on each wheel (attached to two spokes) and one behind the seat. New bikes come with reflectors; if you buy a secondhand bike or inherit a hand-me-down, please make sure this safety equipment is on the bike before you ride.

Lights. Bike shops sell headlights that you can mount onto the handlebars or the head tube. Some riders also wear a flashing light on their backs or below the seat post to alert drivers and other cyclists — it's hard to miss it as it blinks on and off!

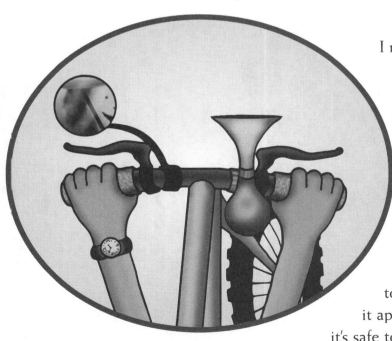

HONK! HONK!

I recommend you mount a bell or horn on the handlebars of your bike. You can ring the bell or toot the horn when you approach pedestrians or other bikers that you'd like to pass to make sure they know you're coming up behind them.

WHO'S BEHIND ME?

If you do any cycling on the road (page 15), you should have a side-view mirror attached to your handlebars. It allows you to see traffic as it approaches from the rear, so you'll know when it's safe to pass a slower rider.

RULES OF THE ROAD

Who rules the road? You may feel as if you do when you're zooming along, but the truth is you're sharing sidewalks and bike paths with other cyclists, as well as with pedestrians, skateboarders, scooters, and roller bladers, so there needs to be give and take. Observing the "rules of the road" will make a you a safe and courteous cyclist!

RIDING ON SIDEWALKS AND BIKE PATHS

The basic rule here is: **Always stay to the right.** If everyone traveling in the same direction stays close to the right-hand edge, collisions and accidents are much less likely to happen.

Although riding on the sidewalk keeps you out of the flow of traffic, be aware that it's difficult for cars to see you at intersections and driveways and it's also dangerous for pedestrians. In fact, sidewalk riding is prohibited in the business districts of many cities and towns.

Passing someone who's coming toward you

One of the joys of riding a bicycle is that it is virtually silent as it moves. Other people sometimes can't hear you coming along, however. If you can, try to briefly make eye contact with people passing in the opposite direction. That will remind them to move back to *their* right if they've drifted to the middle of the sidewalk or bike path.

If a cyclist appears to be lost in thought and is drifting toward you, make some noise so she knows you're coming. Ring your bell, whistle (with your mouth or carry one around your neck), or just call out something like, "Coming toward you!" This way, she can move back over so you can pass each other safely.

Passing someone from behind

When you come up behind someone who is traveling more slowly than you are, you may choose to pass him.

1. Look ahead to make sure that there are no obstacles, such as another road, a pothole, oncoming pedestrians or cyclists, or a car backing out of or turning into a driveway.

2. Let the person know that you are coming up behind him by making some noise with a bell, whistle, or your voice. One common phrase that cyclists call out is, "On your left," to indicate to the other cyclist or pedestrian that you are planning on passing him on the left side.

3. Check your side-view mirror or glance over your shoulder to make sure no one is coming up behind you.

If the situation is clear, go ahead and pass, then be sure to move back over to the right.

If the person in front of you is traveling the same speed as you, make sure you keep a safe distance behind him (at least the length of three bicycles) in case he stops abruptly so that you will have enough time to go around him or to stop yourself.

CARS IN DRIVEWAYS

It's important to pay attention to the cars parked in driveways to make sure that they are not about to drive out onto the road. If someone is seated in the driver's seat, slow down and proceed carefully.

If the car's engine is running and the white reverse lights are lit up, the car is in reverse and is ready to move. Stop your bike and pass behind the car *only* after you make eye contact with the driver and she signals you on.

If the car is moving forward to pull out of the driveway, stop your bike and wait for it to pass. If it's not moving yet, wait for the driver to signal you to go before passing in front of the car. It may be difficult for the driver to see you or she may be completely focused on the traffic or in a hurry and not even notice you.

Also watch for cars turning from the road *into* driveways. Again, stop, make eye contact with the driver and get the signal to go before proceeding.

HAND SIGNALS

Here are three easy-to-remember hand signals that will clearly indicate what you are intending to do. Remember — always look *both ways* before you make your turn.

This motion indicates you want to turn left.

This motion indicates you want to turn right.

This motion indicates that you are stopping.

RIDING ON THE ROAD

Your parents or another adult will determine the age at which you're allowed to ride in traffic and where you're allowed to go. Please speak with them so you're absolutely clear on your household's rules about street riding before attempting it on your own! Plus, bikes are considered to be vehicles, so to ride in the street, you'll need to learn and follow all the traffic signs and laws, just as if you were driving a car.

As you get older and become a more experienced rider, you'll probably find that you enjoy riding on the road quite a bit. It is generally smoother than a sidewalk and you'll have much more freedom about where you can go. There are some areas, however, where no one, even an adult, should be riding, so check it out with an adult before you ride to a new place.

BEFORE·EVERY·RIDE SAFETY CHECKLIST

Keeping your bike safe for riding means keeping it in good repair. In addition to regular tune-ups (page 37), you need to check certain parts of the bike more frequently. Here are the items you should check before every ride:

🚲 **Tire pressure.** You can get a rough idea whether you need to pump more air into your tires using your fingers; if you can pinch the tire, it needs air. But I recommend you use a pressure gauge; you'll get a more exact reading. To check the pressure and add air, see page 18.

🚲 **Wheels.** Hold one end of the bike in the air and give the wheel a spin. Make sure the wheel turns freely without hitting the brake pads or frame. If it doesn't, center the brakes (page 46) or loosen the wheel (page 47) and adjust it so that it's centered between the brake pads. If it is still brushing against the pads, the wheel rim may be warped. Have a bike shop "true" the wheel (adjust the spoke tension to make the wheel perfectly round again). As a short-term solution, however, you can adjust the brake tension (page 59) or pads (page 46). Check the quick releases (page 47) to be sure they're tight. Repeat with the other wheel.

🚲 **Tire tread.** Take a quick look at both tires. Remove any large pieces of debris stuck in the treads (they can cause a flat tire). If you see any places where the tire is badly worn on either the treads or the sidewall or has cuts, replace the tire *before* you ride.

TiME FOR a NEW TiRE!!

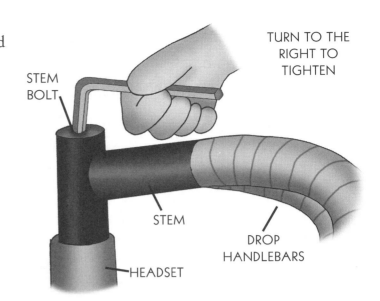

TURN TO THE RIGHT TO TIGHTEN

STEM BOLT

STEM

HEADSET

DROP HANDLEBARS

Handlebars. Make sure that the stem is secured properly. Facing your bike, hold the front wheel between your knees. Try to turn the handlebars to either side. If they move, you need to tighten the stem bolt with an Allen wrench or a socket wrench (older bike models) The wrench size (page 34) will vary among bikes. Also make sure the bolt that secures the handlebars to the stem (not shown here) is tight.

Brakes. If your bike's brakes are controlled with levers on the handlebars, fully depress the right brake lever as you walk your bike. The rear wheel should stop turning and skid along while you walk. If you can squeeze the lever all the way to the handlebars, you should adjust the barrel adjusters (page 57) or the brake tension (page 59). After you make your adjustment, double check that the brake pads don't hit the wheel rims or the tires. To adjust the pads, see page 46.

Repeat with the front brake (the left brake lever) while walking slowly forward.

Gears. Now hop on and ride around a little, shifting quickly through all the gears from lowest to highest. (To review shifting the gears, see page 28). Make sure the shift levers aren't sticking and the chain isn't rubbing; you should be able to move smoothly to the next gear. If you're having trouble, try adjusting the barrel adjusters (page 57) or the derailleur (page 58). Also, check that the chain and gears are free of debris. They should have a metallic shine; if they're dark and grimy, it's tune-up time (page 37).

Repair kit. Do you have your emergency repair kit (page 36) with money and identification? Don't leave home without it!

safety First

INFLATING THE TIRES

Whether you're checking your tires before you go out for a ride or changing a tube because of a flat tire (page 53), you'll need to know how to inflate a tire to the correct pressure. A tire pump that includes a gauge is a great investment — it's much easier to use than a separate tire pressure gauge.

what you need

- 🚲 Floor pump or frame pump
- 🚲 Tire pressure gauge (if the pump isn't equipped with one)
- 🚲 Tire lever (optional)

what you do

1. Rest the bike against another object (tree, wall, etc.) or use the kickstand.

2. You will have one of two types of valves: *Schrader* or *Presta*.

For a Schrader valve, unscrew the plastic valve cover to remove it.

For a Presta valve, unscrew and remove the valve cover and loosen the small metal nut with your fingers. Press down on it until you hear air hissing out to make sure the valve isn't stuck.

SCHRADER VALVE

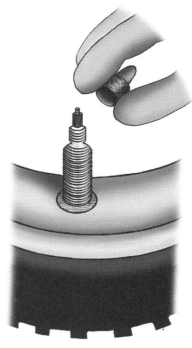

PRESTA VALVE

I've been noticing that it's harder and harder to get up speed on my bike, so even a short ride is turning into a real workout. Whew! What's going on?

Check the pressure in those tires! Inside the tire is a rubber tube, and air slowly leaks out of the tube over time (that's normal). When your tires are low on air, they drag more on the ground, so you have to put more and more energy into pedaling. Also, underinflated tires go flat more easily.

Checking the tire pressure and putting air in the tires is an excellent habit to get into before every ride, no matter how often you ride. You'll be amazed at how much easier and more comfortable riding will be — and your tires will last longer, too!

3. If your pump has a pressure gauge, lock the pump nozzle onto the valve stem (page 20, step 5). With a Presta valve, you'll have to start pumping before the pressure registers on the gauge.

This tire is inflated at 100 psi/690 kPa (typical for a road bike).

If you are using a separate tire-pressure gauge, put it on the valve as shown and take a reading.

Center the gauge over the stem and press the gauge firmly on the valve.

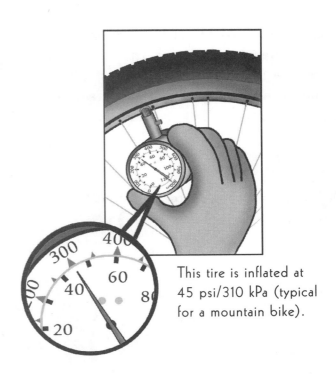

This tire is inflated at 45 psi/310 kPa (typical for a mountain bike).

4. After you've read the pressure, compare it with the correct tire pressure (it appears on the tire wall). The air pressure reading is in *psi* (pounds per square inch) or *kPa* (kilopascals).

If you hear air hissing out of the valve, you don't have the pump nozzle or gauge on evenly and you won't get a proper reading. Take it off and try again. If necessary, ask an adult for help before you let too much air out of the tire!

The correct pressure appears on the tire wall.

5. If you need air, place the pump nozzle over the valve stem (if you haven't already done so to measure the pressure), press down firmly, and lift up the metal tab to lock the nozzle onto the stem.

LIFT THIS TAB TO LOCK THE NOZZLE IN PLACE

6. Start pumping. If your pump has a pressure gauge, check the tire pressure occasionally (with a Schrader valve, you'll have to stop pumping). If not, feel the tire as you inflate it. Don't remove the pump until the tire is inflated to the point where it is difficult to depress it with your fingers.

7. Check the pressure again with the gauge. If you have overinflated the tire, depress the valve (a tire lever is handy for this) or press down on the pin in the center of the valve stem to release some air. Recheck the pressure.

8. Replace the caps, tightening the nut on the Presta valve first.

GAUGES AND PUMPS

* Use a pressure gauge made for a bicycle; tire gauges for cars typically only register up to 50 psi (344 kPa), not high enough for every bike tire.

* A *frame pump* (a tire pump that attaches to the bike's frame) is handy for filling on the road, but to conveniently fill a tire to the proper pressure, nothing beats a floor pump.

* I don't recommend filling bike tires with a service station air hose. It delivers a large, rapid burst of air, raising the pressure so quickly that it can easily cause a blowout. If you must fill up at a service station, add air in short, measured amounts rather than one consecutive flow of air. To inflate a Presta valve with an air hose, you'll need a Presta adapter.

GETTING TO KNOW YOUR BIKE

There are three classes of bicycles: single-gear bikes, road bikes, and mountain bikes. Each has special features designed for particular riding conditions, but all three have many parts in common, too. Aside from the fact that it's useful to be able to refer to the parts of your bike correctly (especially if you need to describe a problem), it's helpful to understand what certain parts are designed to do, and how to use them most effectively. That way, you can get the most out of the bike you already own or compare features of bikes you might be considering buying. To learn the parts of a road bike, see pages 24 to 25; for a mountain bike, see pages 26 to 27.

SINGLE-GEAR BIKES

This basic bicycle is the "two-wheeler" on which most of us learned to ride. There's only one gear, so you don't have to worry about changing gears. The brakes are controlled either by pedaling backwards or by squeezing a lever on the handlebars.

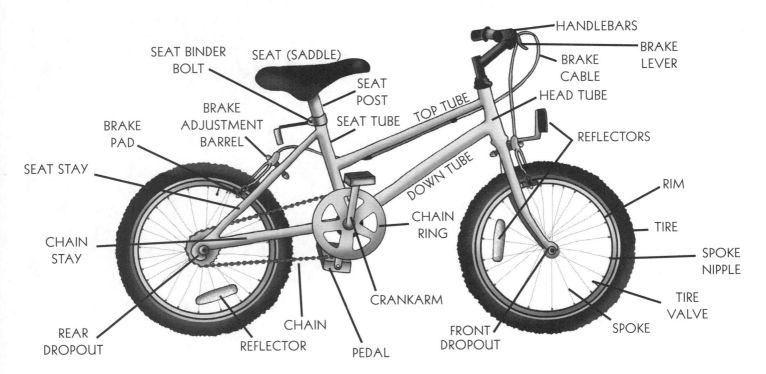

ROAD BIKES

The road bike is the bicycle of choice for people riding long distances as well as those who ride their bikes to work every day. It is also the bike that professional cyclists use for racing.

The road bike is designed to maximize speed. The wheels and tires are extremely thin with minimal *tread* (grooves in the tire so you won't slip on loose surfaces). The smooth tires mean less *friction* (the tire rubbing against the road) to slow the bike down. A road bike's handlebar, often referred to as a *drop handlebar*, is curved so you lean forward when you're riding, out of the direct path of the wind. With your body in this *aerodynamic* position (efficient in relation to the airflow), you can travel faster and more easily. (You know how it's easier to walk into a stiff breeze if you're leaning forward? Well, it works the same way on a bike.) Riding a road bike is lots of fun!

LE TOUR DE FRANCE TURNS 100!

Lance Armstrong (U.S.) leads the pack as the cyclists climb through the Alps. Armstrong has won the Tour de France for four consecutive years (1999 to 2002).

Unquestionably the most famous bike race in the world, *le Tour de France* gets its name ("the Tour of France") from the fact that it goes literally all over the country — from Paris to the south and back up north again. Every July, teams of riders from different countries compete for about three weeks, covering more than 2,000 miles (3,220 km)! (The riders do get a couple of rest days in there!) The race is ridden in stages (typically 20) that cover a variety of terrains, testing speed, endurance, and teamwork.

The rigorous course always includes a grueling section through the Alps, with steep mountain climbs and hairpin curves. In 2003, the Tour de France celebrated its centennial (its 100th birthday)! Check out the race at the official website **<www.letour.fr/indexus.html>.** And then watch some of it on TV, too!

MOUNTAIN BIKES

A third type of bicycle is the mountain bike. It's designed for use on unpaved roads as well as for off-road riding (paths, trails, or open areas). However, more and more kids are now riding mountain bikes on regular roads.

This bike has wider tires and wheels and deeper tire treads than a road bike. The tires can effectively grip the trail and they absorb bumps better than a road-bike tire. The rider sits upright so she can more comfortably absorb impacts when the front tire travels over rough terrain. Also, with the higher handlebar design, an experienced mountain biker can actually lift the front tire over larger obstacles, like a rock, without losing her balance. Some mountain bikes come with *shocks* in the front and sometimes the rear, too. They work just like a big spring, helping to absorb the bumps of a rough, uneven surface.

RUGGED RACES FOR A RUGGED BIKE

Can you imagine racing your bike down a ski slope at speeds of up to 111 mph (178 km)? Or competing in "trials," obstacle courses that include logs, boulders, and water ditches where the fewer "dabs" (when your foot touches the ground), the better your score? If so, maybe someday you'll compete in one of the two big international mountain bike races, the *World Mountain Bike Championships* and the *World Cup*. The cross-country and downhill events feature steep climbs, hairpin turns, near-vertical descents, and spectacular high-speed jumps on a variety of rough, rugged surfaces. Professional mountain bike racers may look like daredevil riders, but they possess a high level of technical skill and control.

Not ready for speeds of 100 mph (169 km) and hairpin turns? You can still have a blast racing your mountain bike at family "fun rides." You don't need a fancy bike or special equipment; the only thing required is — you guessed it — a bike helmet. For upcoming events, check at your local bike shop or at **<www.usacycling.org>.**

Many riders, like this contestant in a recent World Cup event, wear body padding and special helmets on the especially rough mountain bike courses.

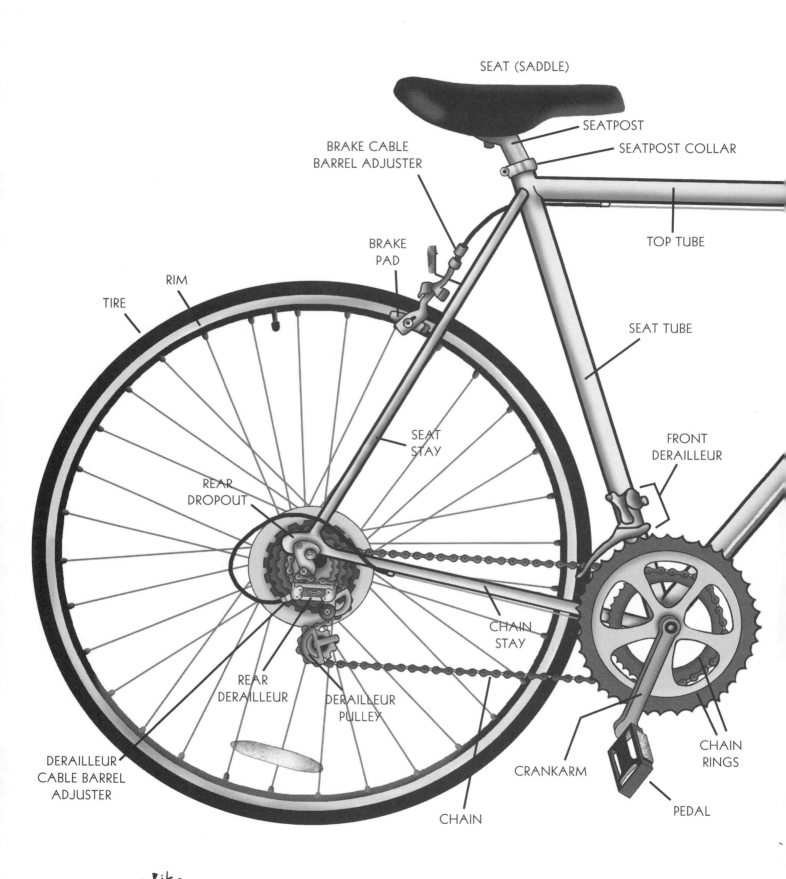

SEAT (SADDLE)

SEATPOST

SEATPOST COLLAR

TOP TUBE

BRAKE CABLE
BARREL ADJUSTER

BRAKE
PAD

RIM

TIRE

SEAT TUBE

SEAT
STAY

FRONT
DERAILLEUR

REAR
DROPOUT

CHAIN
STAY

REAR
DERAILLEUR

DERAILLEUR
PULLEY

CHAIN
RINGS

DERAILLEUR
CABLE BARREL
ADJUSTER

CRANKARM

CHAIN

PEDAL

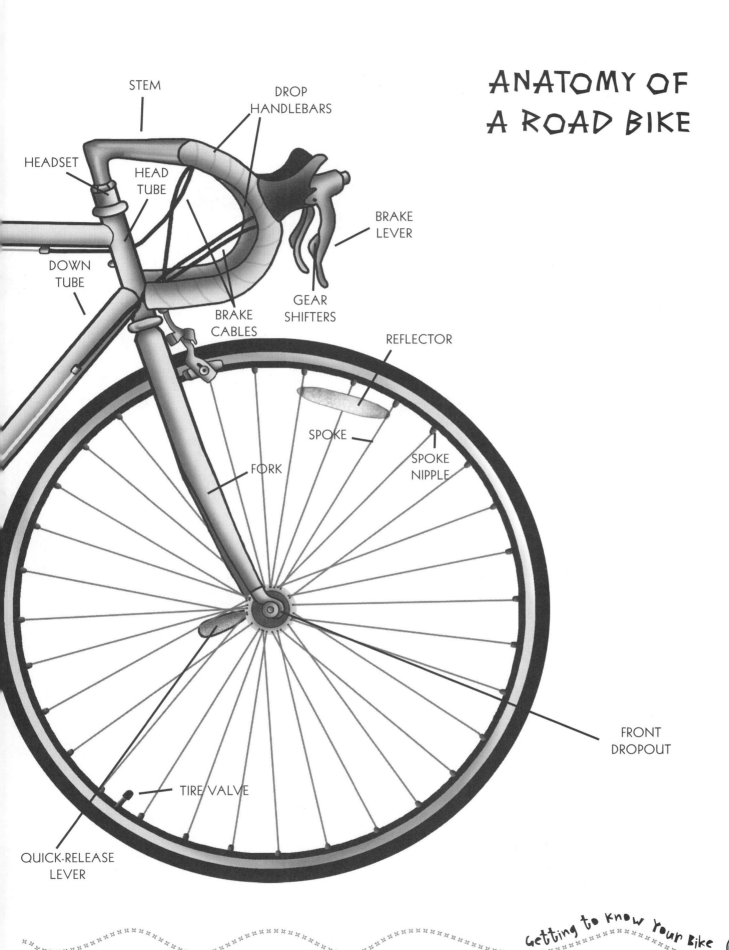

ANATOMY OF A ROAD BIKE

STEM

DROP HANDLEBARS

HEADSET

HEAD TUBE

DOWN TUBE

BRAKE LEVER

BRAKE CABLES

GEAR SHIFTERS

REFLECTOR

SPOKE

SPOKE NIPPLE

FORK

FRONT DROPOUT

TIRE VALVE

QUICK-RELEASE LEVER

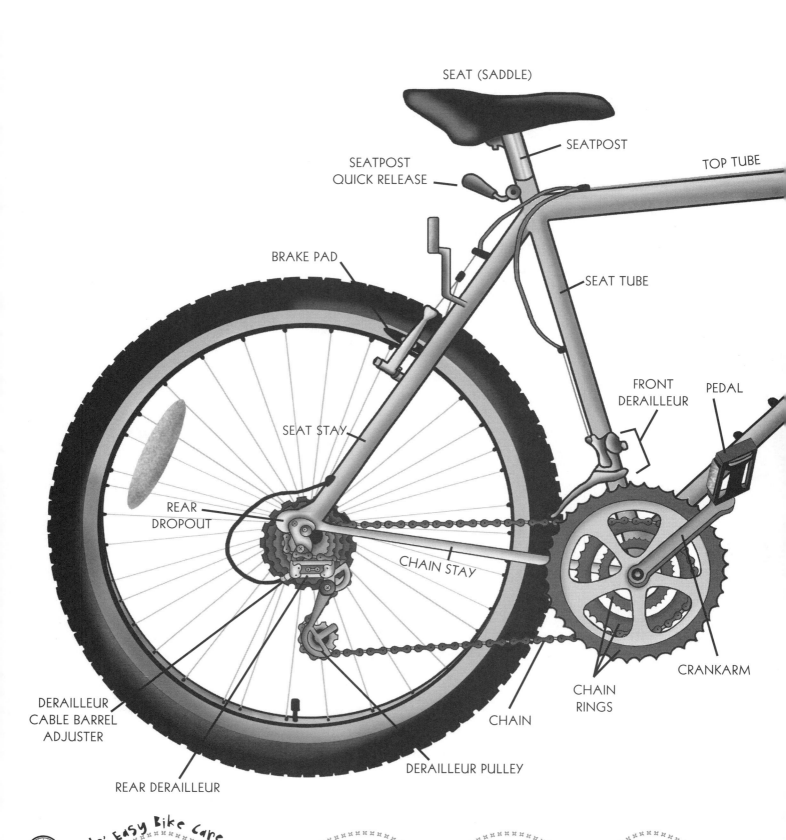

SEAT (SADDLE)

SEATPOST

TOP TUBE

SEATPOST
QUICK RELEASE

SEAT TUBE

BRAKE PAD

FRONT
DERAILLEUR

PEDAL

SEAT STAY

REAR
DROPOUT

CHAIN STAY

CRANKARM

DERAILLEUR
CABLE BARREL
ADJUSTER

CHAIN
RINGS

CHAIN

REAR DERAILLEUR

DERAILLEUR PULLEY

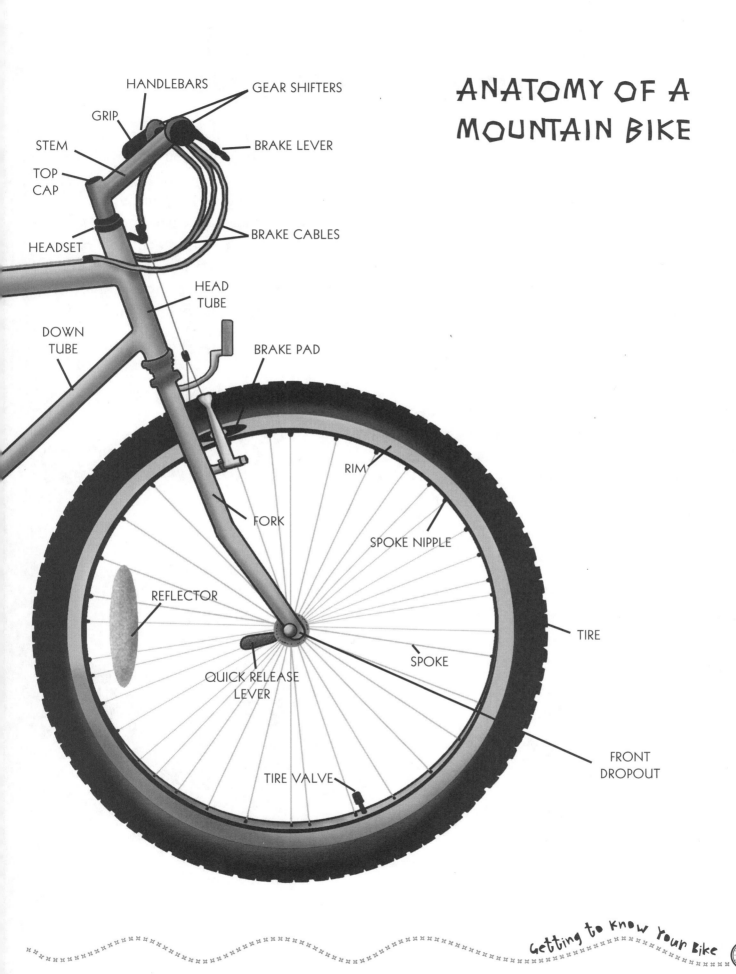

HANDLEBARS

GEAR SHIFTERS

GRIP

BRAKE LEVER

STEM

TOP CAP

HEADSET

BRAKE CABLES

HEAD TUBE

DOWN TUBE

BRAKE PAD

RIM

FORK

SPOKE NIPPLE

REFLECTOR

TIRE

QUICK RELEASE LEVER

SPOKE

TIRE VALVE

FRONT DROPOUT

ANATOMY OF A MOUNTAIN BIKE

HOW *DO* THOSE GEARS WORK, ANYWAY?

As you read through this section, I'd recommend looking at your own bike along with the illustrations. Or better yet, have a friend read these sections aloud to you while you ride around and shift — then I guarantee it will make sense! Your bike's components (such as the gear shifters) may not look exactly the same as the ones shown here, but they'll function the same way.

When you shift gears, you adjust the tension of a wire cable, causing the front or rear *derailleur* (dee-RAIL-ers) to move the chain to a different sprocket in the rear or a different chain ring (basically a big sprocket) in the front. (Derailleur comes from a French word meaning to derail, or to take off a track.) Most new bikes come with an *indexed* gear system. You just move the gear lever a notch (or a click) each time you want to change gears and the indexer does the hard part — you don't need to find the correct cable tension as you do on older bike models.

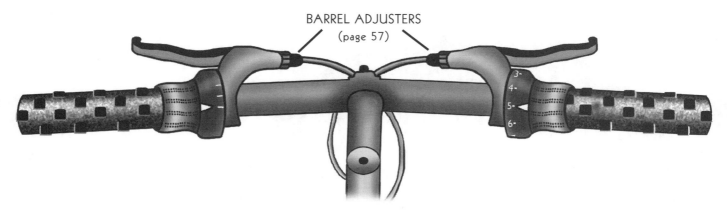

BARREL ADJUSTERS
(page 57)

The *grip shifters* on this mountain bike are easy to use because they're right on the handlebars. Other styles includes *thumb shifters* (small levers that you push with your thumbs).

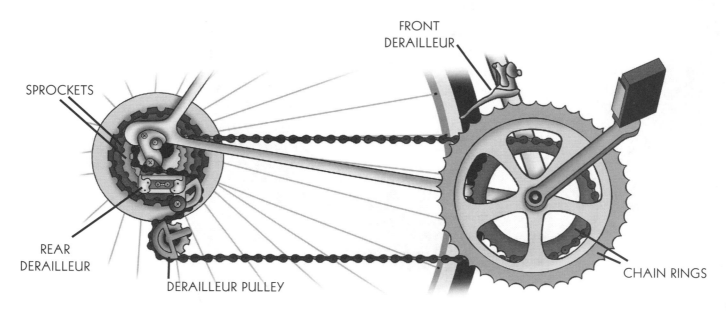

FRONT DERAILLEUR

SPROCKETS

REAR DERAILLEUR

DERAILLEUR PULLEY

CHAIN RINGS

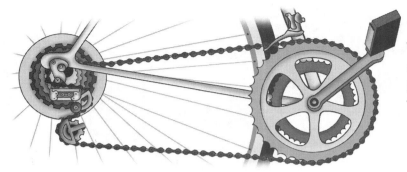

WHEN YOU'RE IN YOUR HIGHEST GEAR (GREATEST SPEED), YOU'RE ON THE SMALLEST SPROCKET IN THE REAR AND THE LARGEST CHAIN RING IN THE FRONT.

YOUR LOWEST GEAR (STEEP HILLS) IS YOUR LARGEST SPROCKET IN THE REAR AND THE SMALLEST CHAIN RING IN THE FRONT.

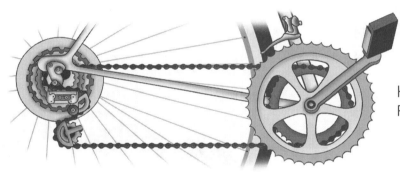

HERE'S A MIDRANGE GEAR FOR VARIED CONDITIONS.

GEARING UP! (OR DOWN!)

* Shifting between the smaller sprockets in the rear makes a small change, so use those gears for fine-tuning.

* Shifting between the larger chain rings (front) will make a major change in the ease or difficulty of pedaling; it's the equivalent of shifting several gears in the rear.

* In the rear, the *smaller* the sprocket you're on, the *harder* it is to pedal. You have to put in more effort to turn a smaller sprocket, but you'll go faster and farther with each pedal revolution.

* It's the opposite up front: The *smaller* the chain ring you're on, the *easier* it is to pedal. Your pedaling is faster but requires less effort on your part — just what you want for climbing a hill!

"Righty rear, lefty lead!"

This phrase is a very handy way to remember how levers for both the gears and the brakes work.

* The **right** gear lever shifts the chain on the **rear** sprockets and the **left** gear lever shifts the chain on the **front** chain rings.

* Likewise, the **right** brake lever controls the **rear** brakes and the **left** lever controls the **front** brakes.

Ask the Mechanic

I'll never remember the ups and downs and the back and forth of shifting! Any suggestions?

Gears can be a little tricky to understand. Here's one way to remember: Shifting the chain in toward the bike (downshifting to a lower gear) is for climbing and shifting the chain away from the bike (upshifting to a higher gear) is for speed.

C'mon! The hill isn't that hard!!

SHIFTING AND BRAKING ON HILLS

Riding uphill

🚲 Look ahead at the hill and estimate how many gears you'll need to downshift to make it to the top. (That way, you won't waste any energy shifting and can put all of it into conquering the hill!)

🚲 Downshift a road bike as you approach the hill and start to feel resistance. On a mountain bike, shift to a lower gear *before* you reach the hill (known as preshifting). You could have a lot of trouble trying to downshift once you start to climb.

🚲 For climbing, choose a gear where you pedal fairly quickly — say, once per second. This will allow you to share the work more evenly across each leg and let you accelerate more easily.

🚲 Some riders like to stand up with their weight in front of the seat post to get more power while climbing. Others prefer to stay seated. You can also alternate between sitting down and standing up to use different muscles. Try all the techniques to see what you like best.

QUICK STARTS
TIPS!™

------

sewer grate ahead!

Keep an eye out for the sewer grates with bars parallel to the road. Your tires (especially thin road-bike tires) can get stuck between the grates, causing you to fall or get a flat tire. (But be sure to look carefully all around you before you swerve to avoid it.)

Riding downhill

🚲 On a road bike, you'll get the most speed using the drop handlebar position. After all, you deserve a fast ride down after climbing up!

🚲 On a mountain bike, be sure your hands are positioned on the handlebar so that you can readily reach your brake levers.

🚲 Keep your feet parallel on the pedals and transfer your weight back, pushing your rear to the back of the seat. This position will also ensure that you can safely stop if you need to.

🚲 Use your right brake to gradually slow down your rear wheel (where all your weight should be!) or apply both brakes evenly. If you used only your left brake (which brakes the front wheel), then all the braking pressure would be applied in front of your weight, and you might perform an unintentional cartwheel on your bike!

🚲 If you feel you can't control your speed safely on an extremely steep hill, walk your bike to the bottom of the hill.

Braking in Sand

Sandy areas can be tricky places to apply the brakes. If you press the brake levers suddenly, you'll lock up the wheels and will probably skid (which could lead to losing control of your bike and falling). Instead, apply slight pressure to both brake levers in short bursts.

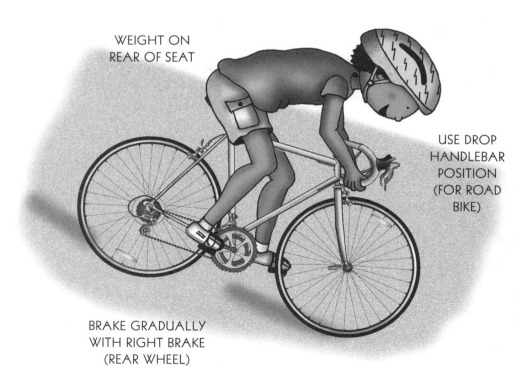

WEIGHT ON
REAR OF SEAT

USE DROP
HANDLEBAR
POSITION
(FOR ROAD
BIKE)

BRAKE GRADUALLY
WITH RIGHT BRAKE
(REAR WHEEL)

TOOLS & SUPPLIES

In order to tune up and do minor repairs on your bike, you'll need a few tools! The good news is, you don't need many, and most of them are very basic, so you probably already have them at home. There are a few specialized supplies that you may need to buy or borrow from another home bike mechanic. It's handy to have a set of tools for at-home maintenance as well as a smaller emergency bike-repair kit that you carry along with you for roadside repairs (page 36).

WHAT YOU NEED: BIKE-MAINTENANCE CHECKLIST

You may not need every size on this list; it will depend on the types of components you have on your bike. To learn about different types of wrenches, see page 34.

- Small slotted (flat-blade) screwdriver, such as a $^3/_{16}$" (4.5 mm) or $^1/_8$" (3 mm)

- #1 Phillips screwdriver

- Socket wrenches (2, 8, 9, 10, 14, and 15 mm)

- Allen wrenches (4, 5, and 6 mm)

- Degreaser

- Grease

- Chain lubricant

- Tire pressure gauge

- Tire pump

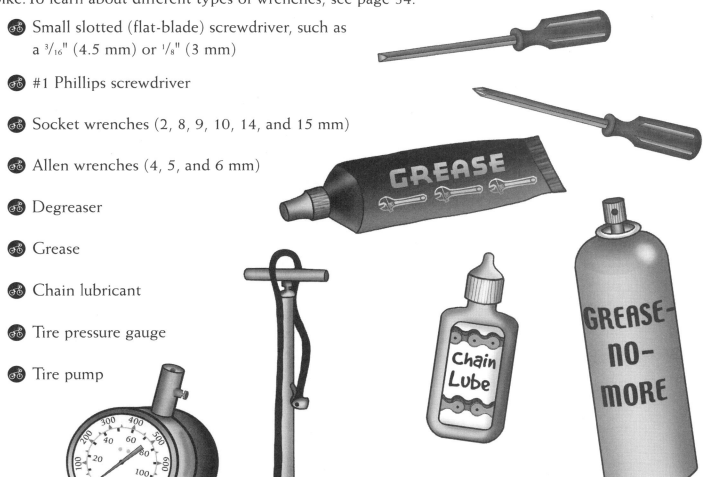

NUT

BOLT

8 MM

9 MM

10 MM

MINI-SOCKET
Y-WRENCH

SOCKETS

SOCKET
WRENCH

DRIVE

FIXED
WRENCHES

THE NUTS & BOLTS OF WRENCHES

A wrench loosens or tightens a *nut* or a *bolt*. Wrenches come in either English (inches) or metric (mm) sizes. Bikes use metric.

A *socket wrench* fits securely over the top of the nut or bolt, giving you the most *leverage* (power for turning). It typically has a handle, or drive, and interchangeable sockets of different sizes. A *mini-socket Y-wrench* has three different-sized sockets.

Where I specify a socket wrench, you can also use the same-sized *fixed wrench* or an *adjustable wrench*. Fixed wrenches have rigid openings, so it's handy to own several different sizes. An adjustable wrench is the most versatile type, but it's also the most likely to slip off as you're turning.

An *Allen wrench* or *Allen key* is also called a *hex wrench* or *hex key* because it fits into the hexagonal (six-sided) hole in the top of an Allen bolt.

ADJUSTABLE
WRENCH

ALLEN
WRENCHES

YOUR OWN TOOLS

Maybe your parents are willing to provide you with a few of your own tools, or you've decided to use your allowance to purchase some. That's great! You'll be able to work on your bike whenever you want. Be sure your folks know that you'll take good care of the tools, labeling them with your name and being careful about loaning them to friends. Plus, you can make a personalized toolbox for storing them (page 35).

Check the hardware store or a large home-supply or department store for lower-quality tools that are less expensive. You can also find great deals on used tools at garage sales. If you have friends who are also interested in cycling and home bike repair, consider purchasing the tools together and sharing them.

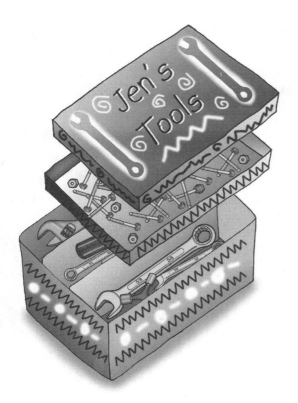

MAKE YOUR OWN BIKE TOOLBOX

You'll look like a real bike pro with this handy kit for storing your tools.

what you need

🚲 Scissors

🚲 Sturdy shoe box with lid

🚲 Cardboard scrap roughly double the size of the larger side of your shoebox

🚲 Ruler

🚲 Lid from a smaller shoe box (optional)

🚲 Pencil

🚲 Masking or duct tape

🚲 Friend (optional)

🚲 Felt or fabric scraps or self-adhesive paper

🚲 Decorations for the outside of the box

what you do

1. Cut the cardboard in half. Trim each piece so it's just slightly smaller all around than the larger side of the box and will fit inside as a divider.

You may also want to shorten the dividers so they're an inch or two (2.5 to 5 cm) below the top of the box. That way, you can set the lid of a smaller shoe box on top of them like a tray (lots of toolboxes have this feature). Use it to store smaller tools and parts.

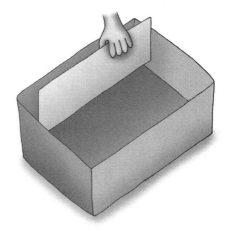

2. Decide where you want the two cardboard dividers (consider the sizes of the tools you'll be storing). Hold each divider in place and mark where it will go. If you're using a small box, you might only want one divider.

3. Cut some lengths of tape so you have them ready. It's helpful to have a friend give you a hand with this part: One of you holds the divider on the mark while the other tapes it in place. Repeat with the other divider.

4. Line the inside of the box with felt, fabric, or self-adhesive paper. Then decorate the outside (don't forget your name!).

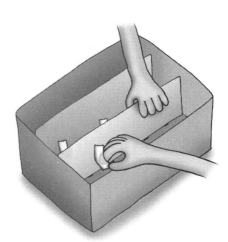

EMERGENCY BIKE-REPAIR KIT

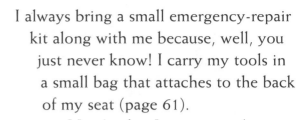

I always bring a small emergency-repair kit along with me because, well, you just never know! I carry my tools in a small bag that attaches to the back of my seat (page 61).

Here's what I recommend you have with you: spare inner tube, tube patch kit (you can buy a pre-assembled one), tire levers, 15 mm fixed wrench (page 34), marker, tire pressure gauge, and a rag. Add a frame pump, identification, and a little money, and you're all set. With these items, you'll be able to fix a flat, not to mention clean the grease off your hands and make a phone call if necessary!

If you pack 5 and 6mm Allen wrenches (page 34), pliers, and a Phillips screwdriver as well, you'll also be able to adjust the brakes and the derailleur (pages 58 to 59) on the road.

Whether you have your own tools at home or not, I strongly recommend that you have your own emergency bike-repair kit so that it will be with you on every ride.

RULES FOR TOOLS

OK, these are pretty obvious, but a reminder never hurts!

* Ask permission before borrowing any tools, whether it's from a family member, friend, or neighbor.

* Take good care of the tools and be sure to return them to their proper places or to the person who loaned them to you as soon as you are through. That way, you'll always be able to borrow them again!

TUNE-UP TIME!

Thanks for the tune-up! Now I'll ride so smooooooth!

An important part of owning a bike is taking good care of it. This means performing regular cleaning and adjustments to keep the bike running smoothly and safely, as well as repairing or replacing broken or worn-out parts. This preventive maintenance actually cuts down on repairs by keeping all the parts in good working condition.

You can do a basic tune-up on your bike yourself, with tools your family probably already owns, plus a few additional supplies from the bike shop. It's fun and very satisfying to work on your own bike, and it can save you some money, too! Why not get together with your biking friends and tune up together? Try sharing the jobs — you might be really good at degreasing and lubing while a friend does a great job replacing brake pads. Then take a spin on those smooth-riding bikes!

WHAT IS A TUNE-UP?

Here's what's typically cleaned, adjusted, or replaced in a bike-shop tune-up:

- general frame cleaning
- degreasing/cleaning of the chain, chain rings, and sprockets
- lubricating the chain, cables, and derailleurs
- checking brake pads for wear; replacing if necessary
- checking the wheels for warping; truing (straightening) or replacing them if necessary

The cool thing is, you can take care of almost all of these steps at home! If your bike doesn't have gears, an overall cleaning and a lubricating of moving parts is still important maintenance that you can do yourself. Of course, it's still a good idea to bring your bike to a bike-repair shop once a year so a professional bike mechanic can check the wheel bearings, inspect cables for wear, and make other more complicated adjustments. A reliable shop won't duplicate the work you've performed. A bike shop can also help you with any of the adjustments in the tune-up shown here.

THE FIVE-STEP TUNE-UP
Step 1: CLEANING THE FRAME

First, let's tackle the easy one — cleaning the bike's frame. It's as simple as it sounds!

what you need

- Old newspapers
- Rags or old towels
- Sponge
- Bucket of warm, soapy water

what you do

1. Spread out the newspapers and turn your bike upside down on them.

2. Working on one section at a time, use the rag or towel to wipe the dust and grime off the frame. Use the sponge and soapy water to clean off any stubborn dirt.

3. With a clean, dry rag or towel, dry the frame so it doesn't rust.

Ask the Mechanic

How often do I need to tune up my bike?

It's a good idea to do a general cleaning and tuning of your bike once a year. People who live in cold climates where they can't ride year-round typically tune up in the spring at the beginning of each riding season. If you ride a lot or in dusty conditions, you might need to do certain parts of the tune-up more frequently. Even if you don't use your bike often, you'll still enjoy the improved ride that a little tweaking and adjusting will give you!

FLIPPING YOUR BIKE

Here's an easy way to turn your bike upside down so you can work on it.

1. Stand on the opposite side from the chain and rest your bike against yourself. Hold the bike as shown.

GRAB THE BACK OF THE SEAT WITH YOUR RIGHT HAND

GRAB THE DOWN TUBE WITH YOUR LEFT HAND

2. Lift and rotate the bike so the wheels swing out and away from you, bracing the bike against your body if necessary.

MOVE YOUR RIGHT HAND TO THE SEAT STAY

3. As the bike comes around, let go of the seat and grab the seat stay. The bike should now be completely upside down.

4. Lower the bike until the seat and handlebars are on the ground. Straighten the handlebars and front wheel so the bike will stay balanced.

Step 2: DEGREASING THE GEARS

The next step is degreasing and cleaning the chain rings and sprockets.

It's important to use the degreaser spray in a well-ventilated area, so work outdoors.

If your chain and gear system has lots of dirt and mud on it, wash it off first with a hose.

what you need

- Disposable gloves
- Degreaser, available at a bike shop (for use with adult help)
- Rags
- Old toothbrush

what you do

1. Wearing the gloves, spray degreaser along the length of the chain and on the chain rings and sprockets.

2. Wipe off those parts with a rag. Be sure to wipe off all four sides of the chain (top, bottom, and both sides), between each chain ring and all the sprocket teeth. "Pedal" the bike with your hands to move the chain along so you can clean its entire length.

SPRAY THE CHAIN RINGS, CHAIN, AND SPROCKETS

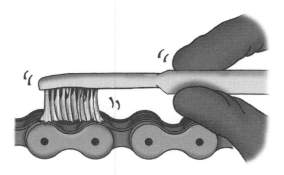

USE TOOTHBRUSH TO CLEAN SPROCKETS
AND BETWEEN CHAIN TEETH

3. Continue to apply the degreaser and clean with the cloth and toothbrush until the chain and gear system loses its dark, dirty color and has a nice metallic *luster* (shine).

4. If you use a petroleum degreaser, allow it to dry before you apply new lubricant. If you use a citrus or other water-based degreaser, you must rinse it off with water and let the parts dry.

STEP 3: LUBING THE CHAIN

Now for some fresh "lube" so that your pedaling is nice and smooth!

what you need

- 🚲 Chain lubricant (available as a liquid or a spray at a hardware store or bike shop)
- 🚲 Rag

I just wiped all the grease *off.* Why do I need to put more on?

You cleaned off the old grease that had dust and dirt mixed in with it. That grit rubs on the moving parts, so you have to work harder to make your bike go. With new, clean chain lubricant, your gears and chain run smoothly — and that means you can put less effort into pedaling!

what you do

1. With your hand, turn the pedal *backward.* As the chain moves, slowly spray or squeeze out a few drops of the lubricant over the top of it until the entire chain is slightly moist.

2. If your bike has gears, pedal *forward* and change gears. Add more lubricant. Continue this process until you've gone through all of the gears.

3. Now, wipe away the excess "lube" with the rag. Presto! You've got a lubed chain and gear system!

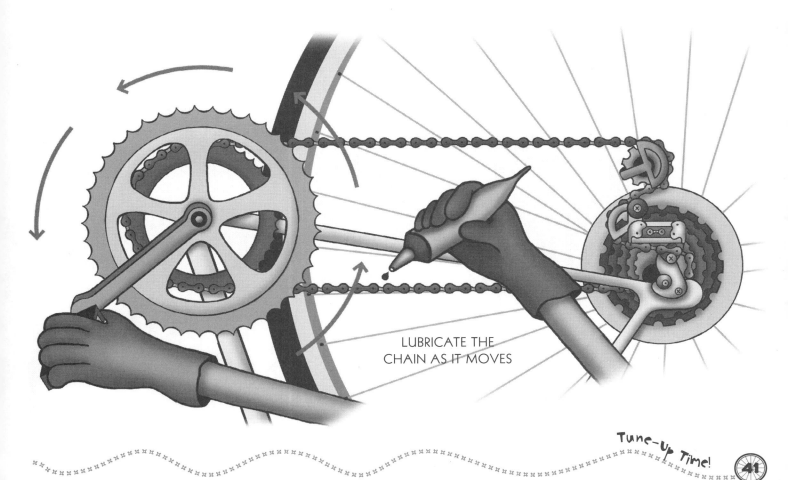

LUBRICATE THE CHAIN AS IT MOVES

Tune-Up Time!

Step 4: CHECKING THE BRAKE PADS

Next, we'll check the brake pads for wear. The brake pads are the most important part of the braking system. They rub against the spinning wheels every time you apply the brakes, and you might not realize how much the friction of those parts rubbing together is wearing down the pads. Worn pads won't grip as well, especially in wet weather. So even if you aren't having any trouble stopping or slowing down, let's check them out.

"Righty tighty, lefty loosey!"

You'll never forget which way to turn a screw again with this handy phrase! Turn to the right (clockwise) to tighten and turn to the left (counterclockwise) to loosen.

what you need

- 🚲 Rag
- 🚲 Bar of soap or isopropyl (rubbing) alcohol and small piece of steel wool
- 🚲 Sandpaper

what you do

1. Remove both wheels (page 47).

2. Inspect all four brake pads. The pads shouldn't be worn to within $1/8$" (2 mm) of the metal backings or the raised rubber lines on the pads.

3. Some pads need to be oriented a certain way. If so, be sure the arrows point in the direction of the wheel rotation.

4. Check the wheel rims to make sure that the metal surface is not extremely *eroded* (worn away). If in doubt, ask a mechanic at a bike shop.

THESE ARROWS POINT IN THE DIRECTION OF THE WHEEL ROTATION

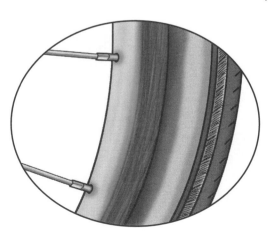

Light erosion grooves like this are normal.

5. If you can see little bits of the brake-pad material on the rims or they feel rubbery or slippery, clean the rims lightly with a little soap or isopropyl alcohol on a piece of steel wool.

If you see any metal from the rims on the pads, rub them lightly with sandpaper to remove it. Roughening the surface of the pads will also help eliminate a squealing problem.

6. If your brake pads don't pass the wear-and-tear inspection described below, move right on to the next part of the tune-up to learn how to replace them!

If they look fine, check the brake pad setup to see if it needs adjusting (page 46).

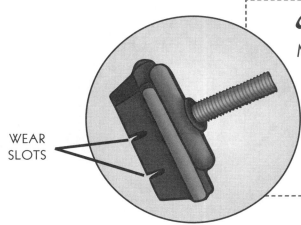

WEAR SLOTS

Check the wear indicator

Most brake pads have a wear line or slots to indicate when they need to be changed. As long as your pads are at least $1/8$" (2 mm) above the line or the wear slots still show, you can still get a few more miles (km) out of the pads!

Ask the Mechanic One brake pad is slightly worn and the other is really worn down. Should I put new pads on both sides or just replace the worn-out one?

Brake pads are sold in pairs, so it makes sense to replace them both at the same time. If one side is wearing more quickly than the other, it indicates the pads are not set up correctly. You'll be checking the setup and aligning the pads as part of replacing them, which will correct this problem on the new pair.

Step 5: REPLACING THE BRAKE PADS

We're almost finished with the tune-up. New brake pads and you'll be ready to roll! The best way to buy replacement pads is to talk to the pros at the local bike shop. Tell them what kind of bike you have and what you use it for, and they'll be able to make a recommendation.

what you need

- 🚲 Wrench (page 34): 5 mm Allen wrench or 9 or 10 mm socket wrench will loosen brake pad assembly on most bikes

- 🚲 Brake pads

- 🚲 2 mm Allen wrench or small slotted screwdriver (to center cantilever brakes)

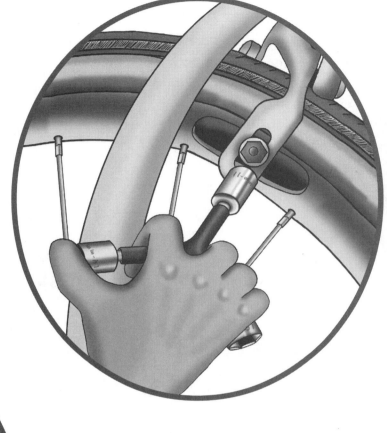

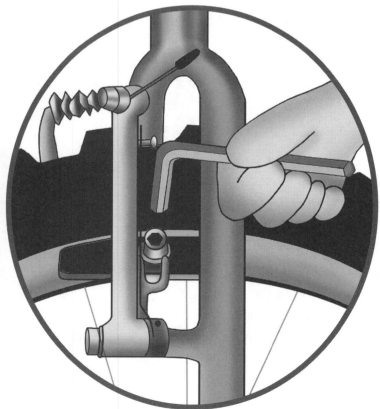

what you do

1. Use the wrench to loosen the nut or bolt that holds the brake pad assembly in place on one side. Here we've shown typical side-pull and cantilever brake assemblies (see pages 51 and 52 to determine which type you have).

Your bike may differ slightly from the illustrations shown with the steps here, but you can use them to determine how to loosen your own brake pads.

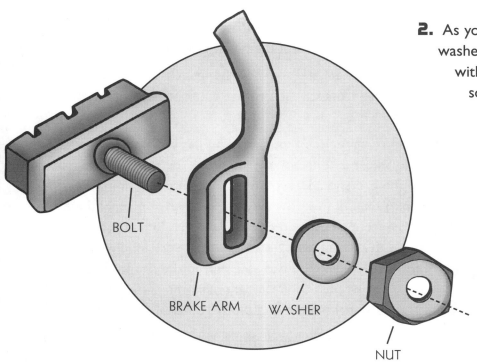

BOLT

BRAKE ARM

WASHER

NUT

Typical side-pull assembly

2. As you loosen the pad assembly, you'll see washers and spacers. Hold onto the pad with one hand as you finish unscrewing so those parts stay in place. As you remove them, set them down in order so you'll know how to put them back on correctly.

Remove the pad from the slot in the brake arm.

Repeat for the brake pad on the other side.

3. Before installing the new pad, check to make sure you have it oriented correctly if necessary (page 42, step 3). Slide the bolt through the brake-arm slot, replacing the washers and spacers in the order in which you found them.

4. Tighten the nut or bolt a little with the wrench until the pad is held in the slot but you can still adjust the pad.

5. Repeat steps 1 through 4 for the pad on the other side.

6. Replace the other set of brake pads, if necessary.

7. Put the wheels back on (pages 49 to 50).

The new pads will be slightly bigger than the old worn ones, so you may have to loosen the brake cable tension (page 57 or page 59) to fit the wheel back on. Now you're ready to adjust the brake pad setup.

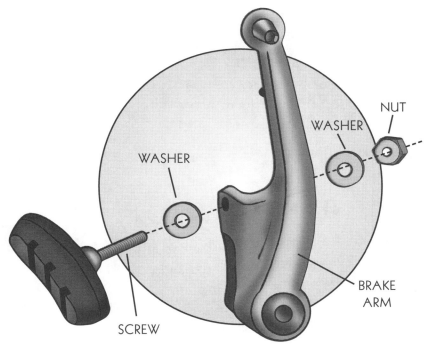

WASHER

WASHER

NUT

BRAKE ARM

SCREW

Typical cantilever assembly

WHEN THE BRAKES ARE
APPLIED, THE PADS
SHOULD LOOK LIKE
THIS ...

... AND
NOT LIKE
THIS.

Adjust the brakes so they are toe-in (step 2)
in the direction in which the wheel turns.

Checking and adjusting the brake pad setup

Now you'll check the positions of the brake pads with the brakes off and on.

1. Spin the front wheel and squeeze the front brake lever. The brake pads should fully contact the rim but *not* touch the tire. Release the brake.

2. If you just replaced the pads, you left the assembly loose so you could adjust it. Your brake pads should be *toe-in* — the front end of the pad should be a tiny bit closer to the rim (about $^1/_{32}$"/1 mm) than the rear of the pad so when you apply the brakes, the front of the pad contacts the rim first. If the pads are toe-in the wrong way, they will squeal very loudly!

Holding the pad assembly in the proper position, use the wrench to finish tightening the pad into place. Adjust and tighten the pad on the other side.

3. Now, without applying the brake, give the wheel a spin. The pads should be parallel to the rim and neither pad should contact it.

If the wheel contacts a pad on one side, check to see if the wheel is centered in the frame. If not, loosen the wheel and re-center it.

You can also re-center the brakes on the wheel. On side-pull brakes, loosen the brake caliper anchor bolt (page 51) with the 10 mm socket wrench just enough so you can pivot the entire unit back and forth to center it and then retighten it. On most cantilever brakes, look for a small screw on one side of the brake arm near the pad assembly. (You'll either need the 2 mm Allen wrench or the small slotted screwdriver.) Loosening it will bring the pad on that side closer to the wheel; tightening it will bring the other pad closer.

If the wheel contacts both pads, you'll need to adjust the brake cable tension (pages 57 and 59).

If you can't get the wheel to spin without rubbing somewhere, the rim may be warped slightly. Have a bike shop adjust it.

4. Now test and adjust the rear brakes.

5. Flip the bike over. Squeeze the brakes *hard* while you rock the bike back and forth *hard*. Recheck all the pads for alignment.

If you have any trouble adjusting the brakes, please have a bike shop check them for you.

Check before you ride!

It's a good idea to ask an adult to double-check the wheels and the brakes to make sure that any wheel nuts are tight, the brake pads are in the correct position and properly tightened and everything is ready to roll. And of course you'll go through the safety checklist (pages 16 to 17) before you ride off!

OFF WITH THE WHEELS!

Turn the bike upside down (page 39). Use these illustrations to determine whether you have *quick-release* or *solid-axle* wheels.

what you need

- 🚲 Socket wrenches (typically 15 mm for the rear and 14 mm for the front) or an adjustable wrench, for solid-axle wheels

- 🚲 Rag (for the rear wheel)

REMOVING THE FRONT WHEEL

For quick-release wheels:

Pull hard to unlock the quick-release lever so it swings freely. You should now be able to lift the axle off the slot and remove the wheel. If not, hold the thumb nut with one hand and give the lever a few spins to release the wheel.

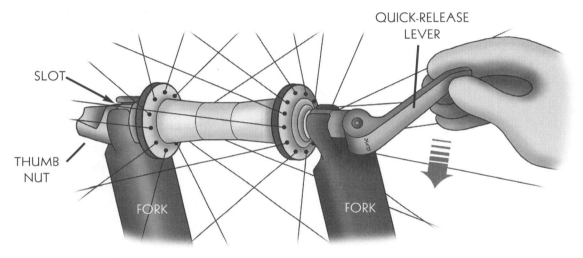

For solid-axle wheels:

Loosen the nuts as shown. Lift the wheel up. If the gap between the brake pads isn't wide enough to clear the wheel, let the air out of the tire or loosen the brakes (page 51).

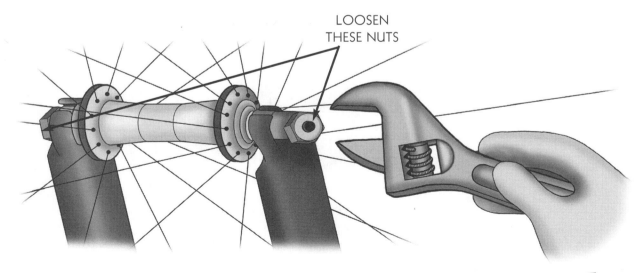

REMOVING THE REAR WHEEL

Removing the rear wheel on a multiple-gear bike is a little tricky because the chain is wrapped around a sprocket.

← PULL WHEEL FORWARD

CHAIN STAY

1. Shift until you are in the highest gear in the rear (the chain is on the smallest sprocket).

2. Let the air out of the tire or loosen the rear brakes (page 51).

3. Release the quick-release lever or nuts securing the wheel (page 47).

4. With your right hand on one of the chain stays to brace the bike, pull the wheel toward the front of the bike as far as possible (until it hits the crossbar of the chain stays).

5. With your right hand, push the rear derailleur backward. The chain cage will pivot out of the way, moving the chain away from the tops of the sprockets. The derailleur can be moved several inches (cm) and may require some force. You should see the entire sprocket when looking from above.

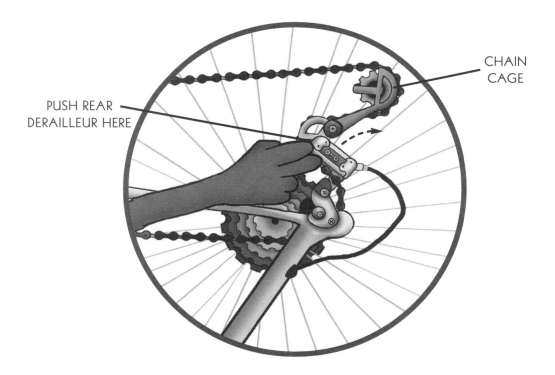

PUSH REAR DERAILLEUR HERE

CHAIN CAGE

6. Lift the wheel straight up with your left hand while holding the derailleur down with your right hand (the chain will be on top of the sprockets). The wheel should lift up easily.

7. With a rag, lift the top section of the chain and move the wheel to the side so that the wheel is free of the chain.

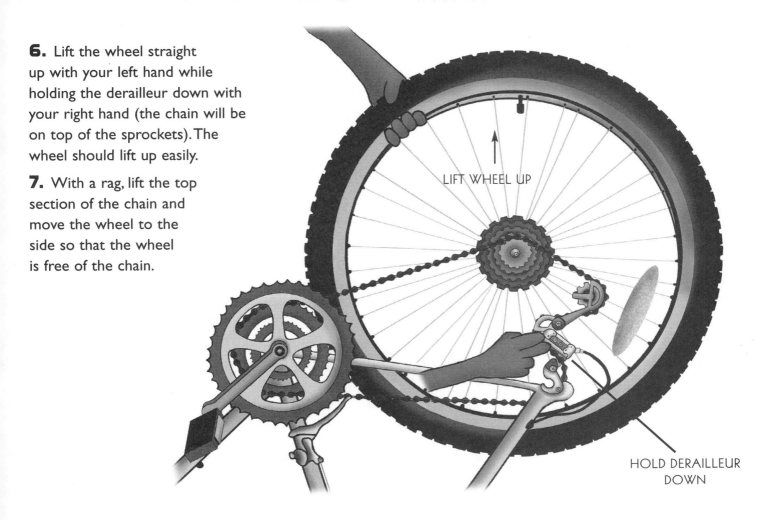

LIFT WHEEL UP

HOLD DERAILLEUR DOWN

REATTACHING THE FRONT WHEEL

Center the wheel in the fork, pressing the axle back onto the slots.

On a solid-axle wheel, tighten the nuts.

On a quick-release wheel, the quick-release lever should start to get tight when it points straight out from bike. Alternate tightening the thumb nut and checking the lever until you reach this point. Then push the lever flat (it should be hard to push). Always lock it against the fork or straight backward; never lock it facing forward; it could get caught on something while you are riding.

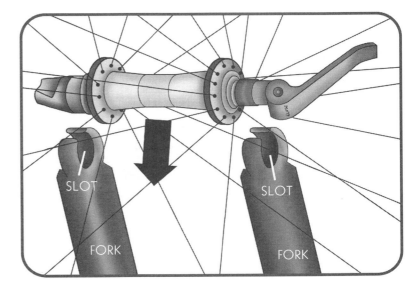

SLOT   SLOT

FORK   FORK

The front wheel should be evenly balanced between the fork.

Tune-Up Time!

REATTACHING THE REAR WHEEL

1. Using the rag, hold up the top portion of the chain with your right hand. With your left hand, position the wheel so that the smallest sprocket is underneath the chain. Release the chain so it drops onto the sprocket.

2. Lower the wheel as far as it can go (the front of the wheel should hit the crossbar of the chain stay and the bottom of the sprocket will hit the rear derailleur).

3. Lift the wheel up by several inches (cm) so that the bottom sprockets are no longer in contact with the derailleur. With your right hand, press the derailleur backward as far as possible (page 49, step 6).

4. With the derailleur pressed down, lower the wheel straight down so that the axle is in front of the slots. Make sure the lower part of the chain catches the bottom of the smallest sprocket.

5. Release the derailleur with your right hand.

6. Using both hands, press the axle into the slots. Tighten the nut or quick-release lever.

7. Keep your right hand on the bolt (opposite side of the quick release lever) and spin the rear wheel forward to make sure it's centered between the chain stays and the brake pads.

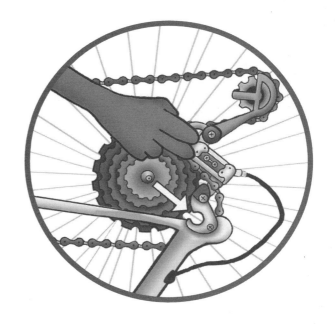

LOOSENING THE BRAKE CABLES

Compare your bike to these illustrations to determine what type of brakes it has so you can see how to release or adjust the cable. Almost all mountain bikes have cantilever brakes; road bikes typically have side-pull brakes.

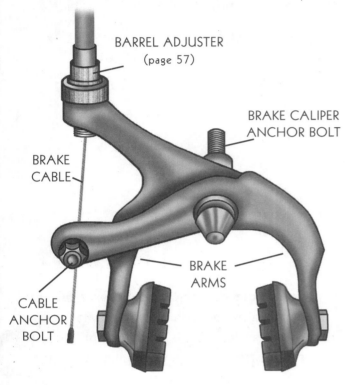

BARREL ADJUSTER
(page 57)

BRAKE CALIPER
ANCHOR BOLT

BRAKE
CABLE

BRAKE
ARMS

CABLE
ANCHOR
BOLT

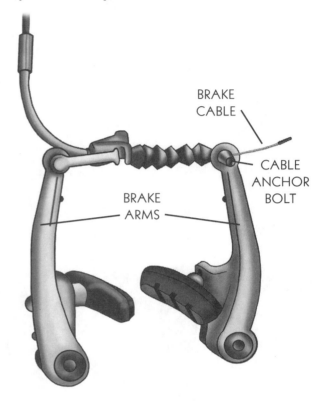

BRAKE
CABLE

CABLE
ANCHOR
BOLT

BRAKE
ARMS

Side-pull brakes require you to loosen the cable anchor bolt on one side of the brake arms to release the cable or to adjust its tension. An 8 or 9 mm socket wrench will usually fit this nut.

Linear-pull cantilever brakes (also called side-pull cantilever) have a cable that runs through a rubber casing and a short metal cable guide and then up to the brake levers.

To release linear-pull cantilever brakes:

1. Facing the metal cable guide, press the brake arm on that side (the arm with the metal hinge) toward the wheel until you can squeeze the brakes together with one hand.

2. With the other hand, hold the metal cable guide where it starts to curve up. Pull the guide toward you and then up. The hinge will drop out of the slot and the brake arm will swing out toward you.

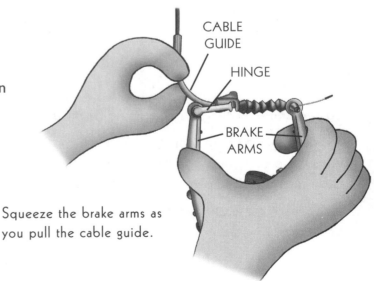

CABLE
GUIDE

HINGE

BRAKE
ARMS

Squeeze the brake arms as you pull the cable guide.

Tune-Up Time!

To reattach linear-pull cantilever brakes (page 51):

1. Grab the tops of both brake arms (start with both hands, if necessary) and squeeze them together.

2. Pull the brake cable toward you so that it's perpendicular to the wheel as shown. Make sure there is an exposed portion of the brake cable facing you.

3. Lift the metal hinge so that the slot on the hinge goes through the exposed portion of the cable.

4. Release the brake cable. Then release the brake arms.

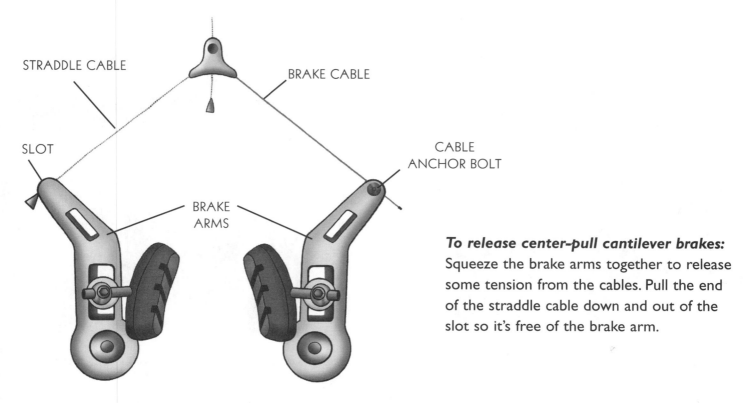

STRADDLE CABLE

BRAKE CABLE

SLOT

CABLE
ANCHOR BOLT

BRAKE
ARMS

To release center-pull cantilever brakes:
Squeeze the brake arms together to release some tension from the cables. Pull the end of the straddle cable down and out of the slot so it's free of the brake arm.

Center-pull cantilever brakes have a *straddle cable* that you release to allow the brake arms to open up so the wheel will fit through.

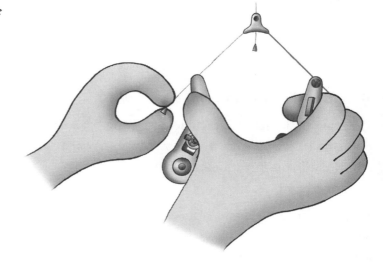

To reattach center-pull cantilever brakes:

1. Squeeze the brake arms together. Pull the end of the cable down so that you can fit the cable into the slot at the end of the brake arm.

2. Release the brake cable. Then release the brake arms.

ROADSIDE REPAIRS

It's a beautiful sunny day, you're riding along with the wind whistling past you … no, wait, that's not the wind, that's the air whistling out of your tire! Uh-oh, you've got a flat! And you're so far from home ….

No need to panic! I'll show you how to fix that flat tire, put the chain back on, and handle other common roadside emergencies such as adjusting the brakes or the derailleur if you're having trouble shifting. The emergency bike-repair kit (page 36) lists everything you'll need. Practice these repairs at home so that if they happen to you or a friend while you're out riding, you'll know just what to do!

FIX THAT FLAT!

Here's how to take the tire off the wheel, repair or replace the *inner tube* (the part that holds the air), and put the tire back on.

If you're just practicing changing the tire, use the end of a tire lever to remove most of the air from the tire first (page 20, step 7).

what you need

- 14 and 15 mm socket wrenches or an adjustable wrench, for a solid-axle wheel (page 47)
- Tire levers
- Marker

- Spare inner tube
- Tube patch kit
- Rag
- Bike pump
- Pressure gauge

what you do

Removing the tire from the rim

1. Remove the wheel (page 47) that has the flat tire.

2. Inspect the tire for evidence of a sharp object that may have penetrated the tire and tube. The tube can be punctured by impact alone and the hole can enlarge after the initial puncture, so you may not see a big hole in the tire.

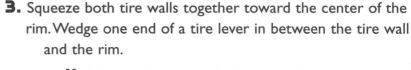

What causes a flat tire?

A flat tire has lost pressure because it is either low on or completely lacking air. How does it happen? Well, remember that inside the tire is a rubber tube full of air. There are many ways for that tube to get a leak. You can run over a sharp stone or a loose nail, for example. And broken glass can easily puncture your tire and tube.

If you're riding a road bike, which has thin tires, avoid hitting hard or sharp objects. Don't ride your bike on or off a curb or over rocks. The pressure from the impact could cause the tube to "pinch," forming two small holes so the tire goes flat. By the way, these impacts can also damage the rim of the wheel, warping it or causing a dent or flat spot. Keeping your tires properly inflated (page 18) will prevent most flats.

3. Squeeze both tire walls together toward the center of the rim. Wedge one end of a tire lever in between the tire wall and the rim.

4. Use the lever to pull the edge of the tire up and over the edge of the rim. You can then secure the tire lever by hooking the end onto one of the spokes.

5. Wedge a second tire lever under the tire wall next to first one and slide the second tire lever around the tire to lift the tire wall entirely over the edge of the rim.

6. Repeat steps 4 and 5 on the opposite side of the tire so that both sides of the tire are out of the rim.

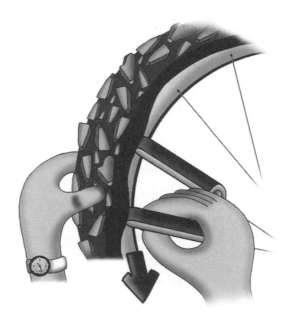

UNTHREAD THIS
RETAINING
RING

7. If you have a Presta valve (page 18), there is a retaining ring that threads around the valve against the inside of the rim. Twist this off with your fingers.

8. Take the tire off the rim and remove the tube.

Finding the hole

1. Now, you'll need to find the leak, which can be a little tricky. Inflate the tube (page 18) and inspect it while listening for air whistling out.

Squeeze different sections of the tube to force air through a hole. Try squirting water from your water bottle on different sections of the tube and watch for the bubbles — they'll show you where air is coming out.

If the hole is more than $1/2$" (1 cm) long or $1/8$" (2 mm) wide, you should replace the tube rather than patching it. If the hole is small enough to be patched, mark it so you won't lose track of it.

2. Look for a matching hole in the tire caused by something sharp stuck in it so you can remove the object.

Replacing the tube

Wrap the new tube around the rim so that the valve is in the right location to fit back through the hole. Then put the tire back on (page 56).

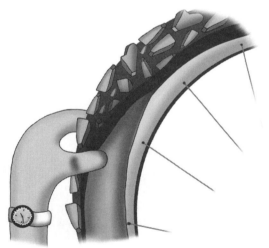

Patching the tube

1. Dry off the tube with a rag.

2. In your tube patch kit, you'll find a small tube of glue, a few square patches, and some sandpaper. Lightly roughen up the area immediately next to the hole with the sandpaper.

3. Apply a thin coat of glue around the hole. Place a patch on top of the glue as shown, pressing firmly on the patch for a few minutes to ensure that it sticks.

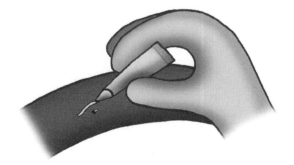

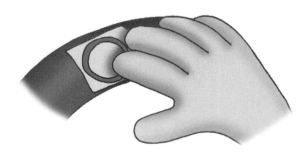

Putting the tire back on

1. Place the tire above the tube around the whole rim as best you can (it's a little tricky).

2. Tuck each side of the tire into the rim while making sure not to crush or twist the tube (this could puncture it).

   The tire won't stay on very well until you have tucked it in about halfway around the rim. Continue as far as you can go using your hands. If you can do the entire tire that way, that's great!

   If not, you may need to use your tire lever again as shown to get the last little bit of tire back into the rim. Just make sure that you don't pinch the tube with the tire lever (you'll puncture it!).

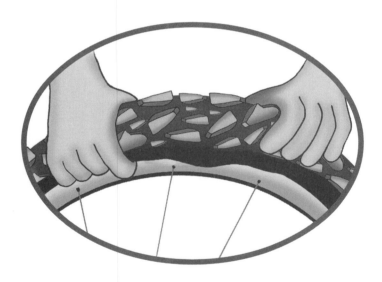

3. Now, pump up the tire (page 18). Reattach the wheel (page 49) and you're ready to roll again!

Be *very* careful not to pinch the tube with the tire lever.

ON WITH THE CHAIN!

Why *does* the chain fall off while you're riding? Well, there could be a problem with one of the derailleurs so that you aren't shifting smoothly, or your gear teeth may be worn out. It's most common for the chain to fall off the front chain ring.

what you need

 Rag

what you do

1. Turn the bike upside down (page 39).

2. If the chain falls inside the innermost chain ring, "pedal" forward to see if the chain will catch on the closest chain ring or sprocket. If it doesn't, upshift in the front (your left shifter) if the chain has fallen inside the chain rings or sprockets or downshift if the chain has fallen outside the chain rings or sprockets. Pedal again to see if it will catch.

Help us! We fell off!

3. Still no luck? Grab the chain with the rag and move it onto the nearest chain ring or sprocket. Pedal forward to move the chain into the gear your shifters are currently set for.

If the chain falls outside the smallest rear sprocket, pedaling forward or backward to get the chain to catch usually doesn't work, so just follow step 3.

ADJUSTING CABLE TENSION

Both your brakes and your derailleurs operate on a system of cables — thin pieces of wire that are tightened to a certain *tension* (tightness). You can easily change this cable tension without any tools by turning the *barrel adjusters,* hollow bolts at the ends of the cable housing, so when you need to adjust either your gears or your brakes, this is the place to start. The barrel adjusters on your brakes allow you to easily adjust the position of the brake pads in relation to the wheel rim. If your chain keeps falling off or the chain skips gears when you shift, use the barrel adjusters to adjust the derailleur cable tension (see page 68 to determine which derailleur cable to adjust).

Here is a typical barrel adjuster; on pages 24, 26, 28, and 51 you can see where some of these adjusters are located on your bike. Screwing the adjuster *in* loosens the cable; screwing it *out* tightens the cable. Adjust by half-turns, then check the tension.

ADJUSTING THE DERAILLEUR

If tweaking the cable tension with the barrel adjusters (page 57) doesn't do the trick, it's time to adjust the derailleur.

Determine whether you're having trouble with the chain staying on the front part of the gear system (the chain rings near the pedals) or the rear part (the sprockets on the rear wheel). Next, determine if the chain is falling off in a high or low gear. Then you're ready to make the adjustment.

what you need

🚲 #1 Phillips screwdriver

REAR DERAILLEUR

FRONT DERAILLEUR

what you do

1. Turn the bike upside down (page 39).

2. Use the two limit stop screws on each derailleur (front and rear) to adjust the gears. If the chain is falling to the outside of a chain ring or sprocket, tighten (turn clockwise) the high limit screws (marked H) on both derailleurs a half-turn. If the chain is falling to the inside of a chain ring or sprocket, tighten the low limit screws (marked L). The screws aren't always marked (especially in front) so you may have to experiment a bit.

3. To check the adjustment you just made, turn the pedals and shift through all your gears. The chain should shift easily between them and stay on the sprockets and chain rings as you pedal. You'll probably have to adjust and then check a few times before you get it just right. Now, you're ready to get back on your bike and ride!

HELP! THOSE GEARS AGAIN ...

If you change the **left** gear shifter so you move to a smaller chain ring (lower gear) and the chain falls to the **inside** of the smallest chain ring, you have a **low-gear** problem in the **front**.

If you change the **left** gear shifter so you move to a larger chain ring (higher gear) and the chain falls to the **outside** of the largest chain ring, you have a **high-gear** problem in the **front**.

If you change the **right** gear shifter so you move to a smaller sprocket (higher gear) and the chain falls to the **outside** of the smallest sprocket, you have a **high-gear** problem in the **rear**.

If you change the **right** gear shifter so you move to a larger sprocket (lower gear) and the chain falls to the **inside** of the largest sprocket, you have a **low-gear** problem in the **rear**.

ADJUSTING THE BRAKES

Let's say you're cycling along and you notice that when you press the brake levers, there isn't very much resistance and you can't slow down quickly enough. Or, you may find that the brakes are overreacting, causing you to stop short. Time to pull over and adjust the brake cable tension. If using the barrel adjusters (page 57) doesn't work, here's another way to adjust the cable.

If you notice that you can't ride as easily as you normally do (and you might hear a noise) because one or both of the brake pads are rubbing against the wheel rim, then you'll need to adjust the position of the brake pads so the wheel can turn freely (page 46).

what you need

🚲 9 or 10 mm socket wrench (center-pull cantilever or side-pull) or 5 mm Allen wrench (linear-pull cantilever)

what you do

Adjusting the brake cable tension

1. Turn the bike upside down (page 39).

2. See the cable that runs from your brake levers on your handlebars directly down to your front brakes and along the top tube back to your rear brakes? The cable anchor bolt screws into this cable. With the wrench, loosen the Allen bolt (linear-pull) or the nut (side-pull or center-pull) so the brake cable becomes slack.

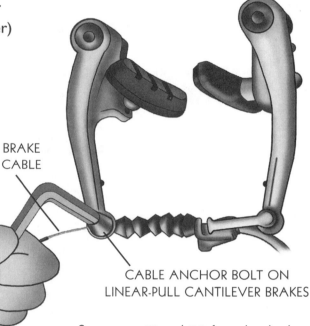

BRAKE CABLE

CABLE ANCHOR BOLT ON LINEAR-PULL CANTILEVER BRAKES

See pages 51 and 52 for other brake styles.

3. Pull the brake cable to the desired tension. You want it tight enough so the brake pads apply a firm pressure to the wheel rim when you squeeze the lever but loose enough to allow the wheel to rotate without rubbing against them.

It's easiest to estimate the tension, tighten the bolt just enough to hold the cable there (don't overtighten it), and then test the brakes as described below.

4. Spin the tire (without depressing the brake levers) to make sure that the brake pads won't rub against the rim while you ride. If the brake pads are rubbing, go back to step 3 and readjust the cable so that it has less tension.

5. Spin the wheel and then depress the brake to get a feel for its response. Continue adjusting the tension and checking for brake response and rubbing until you are completely satisfied! Then retighten the bolt. Be sure to test your brakes (page 46, step 5) before you ride off.

BIKE ACCESSORIES

Want to put a personal "spin" on your bike? Whether you've got a brand-new model or a secondhand set of wheels, you can customize it with accessories to make riding more fun or more convenient. (For safety-related accessories, see page 11.)

WATER ON THE ROAD

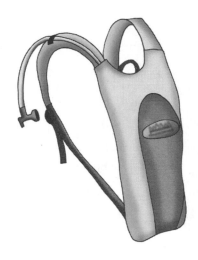

Biking can sure make you thirsty. Even in cool weather, you should always carry water along. You can easily mount a water bottle in a metal holder on the bike frame.

You can also wear your water bottle! A hydration pack, such as a CamelBak, is a special biking backpack that doubles as a water holder. It's designed so you can sip as you cruise along.

LOCK IT UP!

It's an excellent idea to use a bike lock to protect your bike from being stolen. There are several different types.

🚲 **A U-lock** is extremely strong and has a plastic coating so it won't scratch the bike. Many companies guarantee a full refund of the bike's value if your bike is stolen while using their U-lock. The U-lock usually comes with a separate plastic holder that attaches to your bike frame so you can conveniently carry the lock along with you.

🚲 **A cable lock** — a length of thick cable with a combination lock at the end — is the lightest lock (easy to carry with you). Plus, it requires special cutting tools so it's secure.

🚲 **A chain** (some have plastic coatings) with either a combination lock or a key lock is convenient because you can use a long chain to lock up the wheels as well as the frame or to lock several bikes together.

U-LOCK

CABLE LOCK

CHAIN WITH A COMBINATION LOCK

Some of my friends lock their bikes no matter where we are, even if we just go into the corner store to grab a snack. Do you think locking a bike — even for a few minutes — is really necessary?

The unfortunate fact is that bikes can be stolen very easily if they aren't locked up. They aren't like a car, which requires the key to start up the engine even if the doors are unlocked. I recommend that you follow your friends' excellent example and lock your bike up whenever possible to keep it safe and secure.

CARRYING YOUR STUFF

One very handy accessory is a *saddle bag*, a pouch that hangs underneath the seat. Many riders use them to carry an emergency bike-repair kit (page 36) as well as a snack.

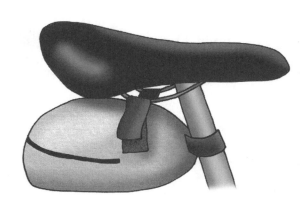

You can also carry gear in a *handlebar* bag.

A *rattrap* (yes, that's really what it's called!) is mounted behind the seat. It has an arm on a spring that snaps down onto whatever you want to carry back there. Great for holding your jacket or your backpack if you don't feel like wearing it, but I don't think I'd try to bring home a dozen eggs in it!

DON'T FORGET YOUR COMPUTER!

Some cyclists use a bike computer (called a *cyclometer*), and you can purchase a fairly inexpensive version. You mount the display on the handlebars and wire it to the wheels. It's fun to track your speed, average speed over the course of a ride, distance traveled, and how long you've been riding as you pedal along!

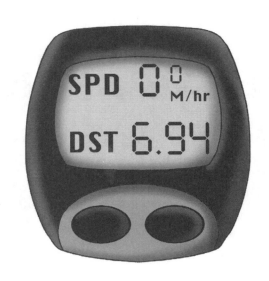

SPD 0 0 M/hr

DST 6.94

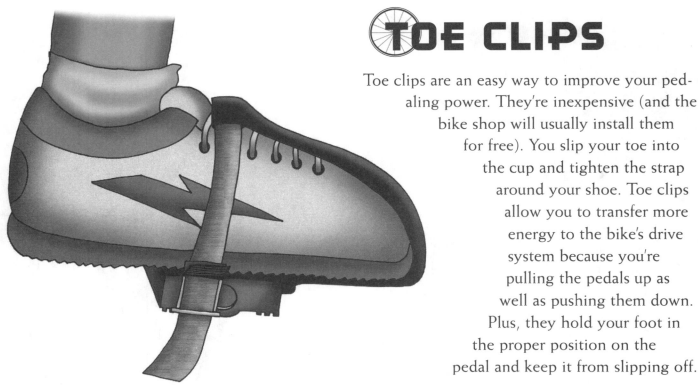

TOE CLIPS

Toe clips are an easy way to improve your pedaling power. They're inexpensive (and the bike shop will usually install them for free). You slip your toe into the cup and tighten the strap around your shoe. Toe clips allow you to transfer more energy to the bike's drive system because you're pulling the pedals up as well as pushing them down. Plus, they hold your foot in the proper position on the pedal and keep it from slipping off.

INDEX

MORE GOOD BOOKS FROM WILLIAMSON PUBLISHING